Glacier Lily

Glacier Lily

poems by

CHUNGMI KIM

RED HEN PRESS ✦ LOS ANGELES

GLACIER LILY
Copyright © 2004 Chungmi Kim

Cover art "Dream" by Vladimir Bourrec
www.vladimir-bourrec.com

Author photo by Mark Turner

Book and cover design by Mark E. Cull

ISBN 1-888996-85-4
Library of Congress Catalog Card Number: 2004090229

The City of Los Angeles Cultural Affairs Department, California Arts Council and the Los Angeles County Arts Commission partially support Red Hen Press.

Red Hen Press
www.redhen.org

First Edition

Printed in Canada

For my husband, Sung M. Lee

For my brother, Jong Sang Kim

Acknowledgments

Grateful acknowledgment is made to the following journals, newspapers, anthologies, and books in which some of these poems previously appeared: *Amerasia Journal, Making Waves* (Beacon Press anthology), *Grand Passion* (Red Winds Books anthology), *Poetry Seattle, San Francisco Examiner, Korean Roots, Korea Times, Inago Anthology of Poetry, dIS★orient, Electrum, Washington State Korean News, Korea Town, Homegrown 2, Malini, One Summer* (Spring Rain Press), *Meeju Catholic Digest, High Performance, Creative Literature, Beyond the Valley of the Contemporary Poets* (Valley Contemporary Press anthology), *KoreAm Journal, Poetry In Motion LA* (Poetry Society of America), *Surfacing Sadness* (Homa & Sekey Books), *Selected Poems by Three Korean-American Poets* (from a special presentation at the Library of Congress), *Between Ourselves* (Houghton Mifflin) and *Chungmi—Selected Poems* (Korean Pioneer Press).

I would like to thank Russell Leong for prodding me for many years to compile my poems for a book and giving me his expert advice. I am deeply grateful to Wanda Coleman and Ronnie Golden for reading my manuscript and giving me invaluable comments; especially, Nan Hunt for introducing me to Red Hen Press and meticulously reading my poems and offering me forthright comments and suggestions. Finally, I would like to acknowledge the support and the encouragement I have received over the years from my fellow writers, Emma Gee, Evelyne Blau, Jan Haag, Donna Frazier and the members of Pacific Asian American Women Writers–West.

Contents

I. In My Homeland

A Girl on the Swing ... 15
The Color of My Dress ... 16
Mama ... 17
Asphyxiation ... 18
My Sister ... 19
Mother/Daughter Dialogue ... 22
Like an Eclipse ... 27
Sorrow ... 30
A Mound of Anger ... 32
In My Homeland ... 33

II. Glacier Lily

Monologue ... 37
Phantoms ... 38
Glacier Lily ... 40
My Sin ... 41
Two Friends ... 42
On the Beach ... 44
Encounter ... 45
My Life with Strangers ... 46
In My Heart ... 49
My Privilege ... 50

III. Some Of Us Are Still Wanderers

Showing Myself ... 53
I Am ... 54
Who Owns the Room? ... 56
A Marginal Being ... 57
Off to the Grammys ... 58
Hollywood Blues ... 60
Betrayal ... 62
My Enemy, Myself ... 64
Chaos ... 66

Being Direct 67
Yellow Rose 68
A Quest 69
My Mazda 70
At the Mountaintop 72
Consolation 73
Humiliation 74
Brother 76
America! 78
Some of Us Are Still Wanderers 81

IV. Passing Love

Epilogue 85
Spare Me 88
Kindly Speaking 89
Remember 90
Love Is 92
Hallucination 94
Dread 96
A Masquerade 98
The Footfall 100
Passing Love 101
A Touch of Love 102
Letting You Go 103

V. One Rock, One Pebble, One Moment

A Seagull 107
In the Sea 108
Santa Ana Winds 109
Ojai Retreat 110
The Scent of an Apple 111
Pink Clouds 112
Huckleberry Picking 113
Haleakala 114
Night Rain in Maui 116

The Autumn Leaves   117
At the Café, Ace of Cups   118
One Rock, One Pebble, One Moment   119

VI. Falling In Love

With You Away   123
One Spring Day   124
Fog Horn   126
In the Shadow   128
Allow Me   129
Autumn by Lake Superior   130
Falling in Love   131
A Private Moment   132
Being in Love   133

VII. As My Life Is A Dream

Reflections in the Window   137
Emptiness   138
Searching   140
The Final Contemplation   141
In a Cycle   142
Living in Dreams   143
The Mirror   144
Summoned   145
In Pure Joy   146
On the Freeway   147
As My Life is a Dream   148
Returning   149
A New Life   150

I

In My Homeland

A Girl on the Swing

She sees the mountain
upside down.

With her long hair
sweeping the fallen leaves
she swings
like a pendulum.

From the lagoon at sunset
a hundred sparrows fly away.

Wishing them back
she whistles softly.
And downward
she falls into the sky.

The Color of My Dress

Looking out the window upstairs in my room
    the color of the bush down the road caught my eyes:
    The light flesh hue of the weedy branch
    the very same color of my dress long ago.

When I was ten, my mother made me a dress.
    Out of silk, she dyed the very same color for
    the August Full Moon Harvest Day. I remember
    the sleepless night waiting for the dawn.

I wore it once, and never again. The war like a wind
    came and stole everything; everything for a mound of ash.
    The dress in the light flesh hue of the weedy branch
    never found me alive since then.

Mama

Brother wrote me a letter the other day that
you were too sad to hold your head up, because
your son was leaving you as I did many years ago.

I ran out into the night and played tennis till late.
The wind swept, and I went on, drinking the air
filled with memories of your silent breath:
The denial of everything you've lived for
for seventy-two long years.

I felt sick on the bench that night and coughed
till dawn. The doctor listened to my lungs and said
it was bronchitis I was suffering from. He never thought
of listening to my heart deeply hidden
in silence as heavy as yours.

Today, Mama
I played the piano with my defiant fingers.
Then the tears poured out onto the keyboard I was pounding
mad. There I saw nothing but your face
your story—

Mama
how did you ever make me this way
never forgetting
the sorrow of your unspoken life?

Asphyxiation

One summer
night of July
in Seoul.

Soaked in sweat
I woke up
three in the morning.

    A cricket chirped
    out loud
    hidden in the court.

I heard my Mother
moaning
all night long.

Through the paper
window
the street light watched us.

    Dreamless
    the heat of the summer
    never went to sleep.

In the darkness
unfolded thin, the dog
whimpered.

Biting his chain
in thirst and pain
he bled till dawn.

My Sister

My Sister
a saint-like woman
I hear you've lost
your beloved son, Taesun.
At twenty
he died of a heart attack
swimming at Tae Neung Pool
Seoul, Korea.

My Sister
a suffering soul
I hear you've lost
your voice over the grief.
At fifty-two
your hair is white as onion roots
and your hands stiff
as an iron rake.

Born a woman
you lived in the shadow
of a madman's kingdom.
You weren't to dance or sing
but to wash and cook.
You weren't to laugh or speak
but to whisper or be silent.
You simply died
when you were born
a woman.

With children growing
you had hopes to live
the life you dreamed of
in secret.
You were courageous
traveling
through the darkest nights
fighting the hunger and cold
for your beloved children.

All the while
the madman in his kingdom sat
on the altar you built
drunk on prestige
shining gold coins
for the ritual he never had.

When you lost your first girl
sweet sixteen
you went mad, tearing
your own flesh against the earth
cemented.

In tears
your baby girl watched you
for many nights.
One day silently she went out
to deposit herself in an asylum.

Only then
slowly you came back to life
turning your cry
into a whispering lullaby.
A prayer of love.

One snowy night
she saw
the vision of her mama calling
and came home.
Back to your nest.

Now your baby boy of twenty
gone forever
you've lost the voice to sing
the soul to dance
the will to live.

O, my Sister
if I ever hear from God
I'd ask Him to give you a smile
to melt the sorrow and anguish
you've long suffered.

If I ever hear from God
I'd ask Him to make you forget
everything in your haunted memories
of the past and bless you
with magic to turn your tears
into pearls.

Mother/Daughter Dialogue

DAUGHTER: I see your face, Mother
smiling
with a shadow behind
in the sunset.

The days of your youth
in your eyes
silently unraveling—

Born a woman
half a century sooner
you were a warrior
in disguise.

Your heart filled
with love and courage
you taught your children
such optimism
that life was indeed worth
the living.

At seventy-seven now
you sit against the wall
your back bent
your body shrunk in half.

Silent in apathy
you do not cry
for joy or sorrow.
And you have no questions
about my homecoming.

Tell me, Mother
what has taken your soul
away?

MOTHER: Nothing matters.
              Nothing—in this life.
              I am waiting
              to be taken away.

DAUGHTER: Why, Mother? Why?

MOTHER: A bride of seventeen—
              I was married to a man of thirty
              chosen by my grandmother.
              The first, the only man.

              He was proud as an eagle
              with a temper like a thunder storm.

DAUGHTER: Did you love Father?

MOTHER: I bore him four sons
              he was proud of.
              I bore him five daughters
              he was indifferent to.
              Together we built a nest of wealth
              and nurtured our children
              with words of wisdom.
              I taught you to respect
              your Father.

              But nothing matters—any more.

DAUGHTER: What anguish do you remember
              most, Mother?

MOTHER: Your brother went to war
              and never returned.
              I never forget—

              Help me, help me, Mother
              he cried. If I go to the war now
              I fear I'd never come back alive.

He knew his destiny.

A box of ashes came home.
And the world around me was
shattered.

One month after his death
the day of liberation came.
Just one month after . . .

DAUGHTER: In another war
you lost your daughter.
My sister.

Born a girl
in the year of the horse
she was the daughter
with a wild temper.

She sang in a voice
sharp as a knife
danced in the night
like the flame of a torch.

Her ambition grew
like grapes on the vine.
But then she was
in disgrace
for being a woman.

The war broke out.
And she flitted
from one illusion to another.

One rainy day
she ironed her dress
with pretense
and drank the water
of sweet death.

A virgin—dead.
At twenty-one.
She was buried
in the wilderness.

In the wilderness
where her virgin soul was
destined to linger eternally.

Mother wailed.
The pain and anguish
nailed hard on her bosom
and rusted in all the years.

Now in apathy—

MOTHER: I prayed to God
prayed to Buddha
to take away my life
instead of my children.

God and Buddha
they left me long ago
when the war broke out.

But nothing matters.

Nothing . . .

DAUGHTER: It matters, Mother.
It matters that you are
my mother.

Through you
I had a vision of life
different from yours.

Through you
I learned the wisdom
to seek for freedom.

You paved the way
for my journey
into the world unknown.

Through you
I gained the courage
to survive.

It matters that I am
your daughter.

Mirror to mirror
through myself I see you.
You see me.

Are you not happy that I came
to see you?

Show me a smile
however faint.
Open your heart
just one more time.

MOTHER: Tears, my tears . . .
Strange . . .
you bring my tears back.

Am I alive?

DAUGHTER: You are, Mother
eternally . . .

Like an Eclipse

In my sleep
the devil licked my guts
making knots up to my throat.

It sat twined
watching me wake up.

Tangled in blurry pain
my fingers refused
to tap dance on the keyboard.

It sat curled up
grinning in triumph.

So I flew on a patch
of white cotton clouds.
A wanderer to be healed.

In the museum
old ladies sat
breathing the dust
of two hundred years.

In an ancient jail
full of empty chairs
the hungry ghosts wove
cobwebs for a meal.

The sun outside
blinded my weary eyes
darkening my heart
like an eclipse.

Last night
my brother on the phone
sputtered words
something about Rina
going back to the asylum.

Rina, don't
please don't sit there
with a devil's smile.

And what about Taesun
my young nephew
robbed of the breath
of life
in an instant
he plunged
with open arms
in joy
plunged
in exultation
loving life
whole-heartedly.
A fool
not knowing
the devil
watching him
with a knot
to strangle him
for a laugh!

The sun in the pool
blinded him
darkening his heart
like an eclipse.

Rina, don't
please don't sit there
with a devil's smile.

Spit out the pain
let your heart burn
in a flame
you'll be reborn.
Reborn.

Forget your baby
forget your man.
Be still, Rina.
Listen.

And live.

Sorrow

When my old friend, Sorrow, visits me
even a small voice calling my name
brings me tears.

Give me one reason why I must see you
tonight, Sorrow.

You come to me, blowing a whistle
piercing the tunnel of my ears
squeezing the age old nihilism
out of every bone of my body

until I kneel and weep.

When you visit me, my Sorrow
I curl up like a little girl.
A little girl who learned the fear of death
long ago in the war.
A little girl who was left alone in the night
crying out, bleeding.

Tonight, my Sorrow
I do not know why you've come to me.
My old days long gone
I have no more nightmares of the war
and no more fear of death.

Only
I am still in search of
loving life.

My Sorrow
you are friend and enemy.

Come
embrace me with your cruelty
break my body in a thousand pieces
and let it be born again.

Like a rock.
I won't know you then.

A Mound of Anger

My mother came to me again
in my dream. She was angry, shouting
a farewell at the doorway.
That night my throat hurt, as if I had drunk
some deadly poison.

I fell ill, coughing up phlegm
yellow puss drained from my head and chest.
Fever ran high while I stayed inside my room
filled with poisonous air of guilt and resentment.
In one moment I trembled from the cold.
In another I perspired like water through a sieve.

Mama, please don't come to me
in my dream! My voice shot into the void.

After consuming forty packages of herbal medicine
at last a mound of anger in me erupted
like a volcano. The fire from it escaped
through my nose, leaving thirty mounds of blisters.
What a bloody mess! Soon the scabs like volcanic
rocks sat under the shade of my nose for two weeks.

My pale yellow face staring at the void
I yelled out a farewell to Mama.
I'm sorry, Mama, I never kept my promise
to take care of you in your old age. Away from home
I've always been your helpless baby, yearning
for your love and care in this foreign land.
Leave me be, Mama. You and I are not inseparable.
I will grow up and let go of you.

Let go of me, Mama. Farewell!

In My Home Land

In hollowness, the sound of the hammering clamors
against the walls of the modern dwelling.

Sweating over the steel rods and the concrete floors
men work silently in the sweltering heat.

The villagers crawl into their dusty houses
dwarfed by the towering shell of a modern apartment
complex.

Once a peaceful and beautiful mountain side
this place on the outskirts of Seoul is now sandwiched
between old and new changing forces.

The children run and scream in the paved parking lot
with no playground.
Choked with dust and noises

the pine trees on the hillside stoop over timidly
intimidated by the sky-reaching cranes.

II

Glacier Lily

Monologue

Imprisoned
in a modern security building
I pay an unfair amount of rent
each month to live like a nun.

I talk of my dreams to the trees
drink plenty of sparkling water
and dance to music
like a flame blowing in the wind.

The telephone is my only friend
mute and dumb. The typewriter is
my guardian grumbling
in a monotonous tone.

When the rain falls at night
the stucco ceiling trembles.
Then I know how lonely I've been
inside my prison.

Out in the hallway, I hear
someone tiptoeing by my door.
Is it the lady with a dog? Or
is it the man with navy blue jeans?

The walls are thick and hollow.
The doors are dark and heavy.
Through the tightly closed window I see
the freeways spread like varicose veins.

Ask my name, lady, and I'll say
I've got a friend in my modern prison.
What's your number, I ask you.
Mine is 1312 at the top south corner.

Call me any time if you wish.
My mute friend will gladly sing.
Make sure, though, not to come in.
My guardian is jealous of everyone.

Phantoms

In isolation I create
phantoms
filling the space around me
with their screams
sighs and glares.

They enter and exit
stealthily
gliding, floating, flying
and often
stealing my breath.

They smile
when I break down in tears.
They dance
when I sit lifelessly.

Oh, how I make them happy
giving up my power
my privilege
to live.

As the sun breaks into the tunnel
of despair
I see
my divine self standing
in the light
outside the realm of isolation.

The phantoms disappear
like a mirage.

At last
I hear the sound of my own
voice
shooting high to the sky
in one big relief.

My life is a story of phantoms
I create!

Glacier Lily

You are a glacier lily
a poet friend once said to me
at a drinking party.

You are a poet
a woman like a glacier lily
existing solely
in the ice-covered mountaintop
lonely
pure and colorless.

Poetry of frustration
you write in such simplicity
in such purity
revealing yourself
as a virgin.

My friend, he said to me
such is not necessarily a virtue
in this world. How to color
yourself as you age alone
is the life-long task.
You need to add colors in you.
Let's drink to that.

I smiled and lifted my glass
to his face and said
It takes one to know.

My Sin

My sin is
an act of cruelty
depriving myself
of worldly desires.

Locked in a rented room
I sit all day, listening
to the murmurs
of many-headed visions.

Cockroaches are
my temporary friends
dwelling
in their underground
castles.

The ocean is
my mother I visit in need
of love
and companionship.
She only listens
to my laughs and cries
like God in presence.

Old wounds
all over again
come
hand in hand
off and on
like jealous friends
wanting
someone else's credit.

Under a lamp in the night
I meet a unicorn
sitting
in my mirror.

Two Friends

A house
abandoned—

a sanctuary
for two friends
in exile
from East and West.

Dark with weather-beaten
green paint
peeling off
the face of the house
wards off
vanity.

There is no flower
in the garden
to welcome strangers.

Love for illusion is
the key to mystery
inside
where the ferns grow
in the bathtub.

On the kitchen table
a bowl of apples
green and red
accented with purple plums
gives joy.

A gift from Heaven.

Room to room
two friends fill
with the rare lives
of their imaginations

building
a whole new planet
in this space.

On the Beach

Breaking into the horizon
the seagulls dance
low.
Slick.

On the sandy beach
Children run
tittering and chattering.

On a swing in the shade
of an oak tree on the hill
a young blonde-haired couple are
sitting
humming a song
America The Beautiful.

I hear the sky whisper to me:
Where are you from, my sad-eyed lady?
Your hair black as raven
your skin pale as a moonlit gourd
don't you have a home
to return to?

On the rock where the sun is warm
I curl up like a snail
writing
one last poem on the ocean wave.

Encounter

All day
the curtain was drawn.
The light dim and low
I pounded the keys of the IBM.

With no one to talk to
I talked to myself
left brain to right.
I laughed to circulate
the air in my lungs.

At dusk
the city was baptized
with the rare gift of rain.
Cold.
Few spectators ran
in and out of doorways.

I found a roomful of poets
cranking up their dreams
eyes meeting through
lashes.

My Life with Strangers

I'm getting used to it
too much so

getting up alone
bathing in the sun stream
washing my dreams and
hanging them neatly
in my drawer.

Stooped over a table
like a wise old woman
I play with the blocks of words
for future references.

Sometimes
things go mad in the reality
chamber of my brain and
my hands never leave the telephone
all day, all evening
calling it a business.

Still, blessed I am

there are times
when the angels sing
making me play the piano
then I see
the deer roam
swans dance
flowers bloom
birds fly—

rabbits and elephants
a unicorn and an owl
plants and woods
even *Chibari* and *Kakssi*
everything
everyone from every square
corner of my place
they all come alive

singing in chorus
the song of glory

dancing in a circle
and
my mother and Virgin Mary
together they smile
upon us.

This is a place.
My kingdom.
Blessed
truly blessed I am

getting used to
being alone.

When the night falls
I meet the strangers
marching
out of my computer.

Men and women
old and young
children
lost and found
the rich and the poor—

I bathe them clean
make them laugh or cry
feed them food for the soul
cure their broken hearts
with passion and compassion.

So, it's good to know that I am
getting used to my life
with the strangers.

They give me life.

In My Heart

The sea rocks on my table have a life of their own.
Not minding my intrusion, they hold
such tranquility in them.

Returning to thirty some years back, at last I see
the stories of many lives stored, layered as in a rock
formation in a canyon.

Intermixed with paths of my life, they are held like rocks
in the loving space of my heart warmer than the sunlight
ready to be revealed.

My Privilege

Under a dim lamp at night
I build a small kingdom, gathering
all my beloved ones of the past
and the present.

The beginning is an end in my story
as the end is a beginning.

Before you come to a resolution
with your own end

> how many more times will you see
> your father counting coins
> your mother stooped over a stove?

> how many more times will you meet
> your family and friends scattered
> over mountains and across oceans?

> how many more seasons will you encounter
> to watch a magnolia in your garden
> blooming in perfection?

> how many more days will it be
> until you fold your limbs
> unable to move one more step?

In my story
you all live forever
like queens and kings

as children in Paradise.

This is my privilege to cherish
under a dim lamp in the night.

III

Some Of Us Are Still Wanderers

Showing Myself

With the sunlight
on my face
I lie
motionless.

An empty hand lands
in my house of mirrors.

I see the strangers
laughing
like ripples in the water.

I am a fish from the river
thrown
in the ocean.

Where is my home?

I Am

A container
I am
empty
for seasons of many
longing souls.

A dreamer
I am
aloof
floating
timelessly.

Question me
no more
where I come
from
where I must
go
between
East and West.

Vapor
I am
no one can
catch
the presence
in a grasp.

Homeless
I am
rootless
I am
free
as the summer
clouds

carrying home
wherever
I
go.

Who Owns the Room?

The winds bustled about
frantic
for the winter carnival.

I washed my garments
by hand
for the summer to come.

I called a friend to play
the tune of autumn sonata.
She said I was only
dreaming.

On pages
I tried to contain the mysteries
of many lives I've cared about
and five ants crawled
making a map of Zen.

In the night
a shadow lingered
like a demon that embraced
nothing of life.

In forlorn hope
I stood
wondering
who owns the room.

A Marginal Being

They call me
a marginal being

an island
between the continents

transplanted
in this Pac Mac culture
from the land of morning calm.

Silent in anguish
in my dreams I speak Korean
to my childhood friends and
English to my new world friends.
In color or black and white.

In my waking hours
I count the time backward
unable to proclaim my rights
to live anywhere
between the two worlds

with fear
I may be stoned to death
by the tribes of two continents
whose plastic smiles and
false promises
poisoned
the last portion of my faith.

Off to the Grammys

The day at last came
to go to the Grammys.

With a borrowed mink coat
and a yellow flower
pinned
on my black silk dress
I walked
like a star
escorted by my man.

Glittering lights
blinding my eyes
I heard the crowd
shouting
as a limousine pulled in.
A star.
A woman in a slinky outfit
slid
like a rattle snake
a smile
pasted like a toothpaste
commercial.

The auditorium was full
with diamonds and silks
tuxedoes and bare shoulders.
Amongst the shouts and whispers
I sat invisible
sunk
in my own fantasy.

Show biz.
Thousands of dreamers gathered
together in a feast

no one saying hello
perfect strangers exchanging
nothing
but prepared smiles.

Glossy painted-faces floated
the music was rocking
the crowd was stomping
crushing
stepping on the flowers.

Spotlights rampant
food plenty
it was the night to go mad.

Ah, why did I ever dream of
stardom?

A pale moon I was
quietly
content to stay
behind.

Hollywood Blues

Let me not remember how
you want me to be happy
in your way.

For more than a decade
I took your world as mine
lived to meet your standards
burning my pillars of security.

Sickened by your over-blown pride
polished aggression and
the calculated affection you're
famous for

now in my little sanctuary
I learn to live an eternity of one gaze
and one breath at a time.

To watch the sky of clouds
the mountain of trees
tonight by mistake I left
my door open.

You sat on my doorstep
with your usual pathetic smile
blowing the whirlwind of anxiety
into my lungs
mirroring the faces I could not forget
without pain.

Oh how my dreams were crushed
and robbed in your world!
Seduced by the beauty you advertised
allured by your schemes and stunts
I lingered around your castles
until I was empty in body and soul.

You are no longer my master.

I want to be happy
in my way.

Betrayal

Sitting in an empty room
wishing for a miracle
I'm like a sinking submarine.

The day is deepening
into the night and my only hope
is to see the breakthrough of
yesterday's pain.

Tell me what I did wrong
that you had to discard me
like an unwanted machine
to be put aside.

I was overly dedicated to my work
serving you. And I asked you
if that was a mistake.
You only laughed.

I wanted to know if my anger
toward your betrayal was justified.
You only said in a vacant voice
that you were sorry.

Driving home through
Laurel Canyon in a thunderstorm
I cried harder than the rain.
That night

standing by my window
I let the rain storm blot out
the life I had carefully drawn
in such a bright color.

When I saw you the next day
I proudly smiled
like a peony blooming at dusk.

My Enemy, Myself

You scare me again
testing
my strength to stand
the ugliness of the hidden side
gilded but
crowded with barbarous noises.

I've come away from you
carrying
my wish between my palms
blessed with time to play
space to heal
in the salty Pacific Ocean.

Passing by
under the Chinese orchid tree
every day I've touched the sky
with my whispers of joy
loving
all God-given living things
in this island of paradise.

Then you sneak in
through the worm-eaten screen
of my old memories
with filthy pollution on your breath
and a sack of vanity in your hand.
You torture my heart with stones
and my head with burning coals

questioning
what I'm going to do
now the time's up to return
empty-handed
to your corrupted gutter
the jungle I fear.

I am a modern woman
loving the city life
nightly
watching the clowns at play
in your tinsel town.

I am a modern woman
with a vision
to serve humanity
for glorious bribes that you are
famous for.
Yet
when the demons push my head
into your vomiting throat
I have no stomach to suck it in.

My hair is growing white
in my roof-sunken shack.
Will there be guests for tea?
Will there be lovers, waiting
for my soul searching journey?
Or, will they all be out
to your belly-full fiesta?

I will come back, no doubt
riding high
in my magic-filled cloud and
demand your smile
upon my arrival
or else
I will glide along
as if you never existed.

All I want is a place
to sit down for a long while
claiming it as my own.

Do not scare me agaim
with your hisses and fusses.

Chaos

I hear myself talk
like a recording of everyday living.

Bits of information on pieces of paper
pile up on my table tops
in my memory bank
scheming to make grand stories
out of them.

In the meantime, my life is scattered
in a hundred directions
storing all the pressure in my veins.
Even in my sleep I am busy running
the show with such dramatic effects
when I wake up, my limbs are stiff
as a skateboard.

I go to the doctor for more tests and
to the chiropractor to align my bones.
I run in the track to strengthen
my heart and lungs.
In addition to my health nut diet
I take a handful of vitamins.

Always busy solving the problems I create
I let the stress build up and retreat to rest.
Thus, my life is spent busy taking care of
my body to undo the stress that I have stored.

Trapped in a low income living
for the sake of freedom
I am gambling my future on dreams.

Still
stiff and painful in my inflamed joints
I yell, condemning my stupidity
for living in chaos.

Being Direct

I told my neighbor
she had no right to ask me to cut down
my garden trees for her benefit.
She never spoke to me again.

I told my doctor
he had no right to make me wait
for hours in the waiting room every time.
He gave me a plastic smile.

I told a sales lady at the store
she had no right to push me aside
because of the color of my skin.
She accused me of insulting.

I told a man of position
he had no right to sit on my resume
for six and a half months with no excuse.
He said he'd never respond to such as mine.

I told a friend who claimed to be truthful
she had no right to betray me
with lies and slanders.
She turned away without a goodbye.

Perhaps, the mistake was that I failed
to lower my eyes, bow deeply and smile
like a demure little Asian girl who was
saved by a white missionary.

Might as well be a monkey
covering my eyes, ears and mouth
keeping my dignity
however fragile it may be.

Yellow Rose

A yellow rose
from Ellen's garden

blooming.

Mesmerized by its beauty
I put it in a vase and
placed it in front of the mirror
in my bathroom.

Each time I encountered it
I showered it
with pretty smiles
as if to make it stay
in full bloom.

The following day
someone's humiliation put me
in a suicidal mood.

I ran into the bathroom
weeping
like a widow at night.

Wilted
the yellow rose dropped
its head in the basin.

The scattered petals
floated
in my tears.

Each petal like an angel's wing
placed me in a halo
of peace and beauty.

A Quest

Every morning you gather
the fragmented dreams of the night
like an unsolvable puzzle

drink a cup of hot carob protein
to feed your organs and
drive like a maniac weaving through
the city boulevards
breathing the poison of anxiety.

Wishing
you were somewhere else
where the sun strokes your face
you converse
with the stream of your silent murmurs
bridging the past and the future.

Three million knots
tangled in the labyrinth of your head
your broken mirrors reflect
the shady corners of your eyes.

When frustration runs through you
like mudslide after the storm
hardening the vessels

you stand in a street of Hollywood
questioning
who you really are . . .

My Mazda

In the stream of afternoon traffic on Hollywood Boulevard
my orange colored Mazda squeaked aloud.
I'm in a rush, don't make trouble, I said. She shook her body
coughing up and spitting out black blue smoke from the tail end.
Damn you! I spat anger crushing down on the clutch.
Get me cured, she said, I'm getting old and sick just as you are.

Oh, Mazda, my dear, this is no time to argue. Take me
to the place where I'm supposed to be. I kicked her stomach
pumping gas into her head. Go! I yelled.

Putt—putt—she coughed, jerking me around at the wheel.
Huffing and puffing like a tired mule, she pulled away.
Slowly giving up, she sat back right before the traffic light.
Oh, Mazda, don't do this to me now. Go. Please go!
Behind me I saw a long line of cars straight down
to the next intersection. Go! Mazda, go! I kicked her hard
but all in vain.

Come, Mazda, I'll take you to get cured. I pumped her up.
There she moved and jerked again throwing me forward.
She pouted. Sorry, Mazda, I hit you too hard. I chuckled.

You, spoiled brat. I've kept you for seven years ever since
you were given to me for my seven year love of labor
by the cheapskate you know who. I've cared for you cleanly
and meticulously always overly concerned, for you were
the master on the road, my servant, my legs. I've poured fortune
into your belly, guarding your heart like a jewel
balancing your head with oil and water. I've cared for you
more than for my own body.

Putt—putt—putt. She whimpered, moving a step forward.
Oh, don't stop, don't—please. Thump!
Mazda, the master of the road sat in the middle of
the two–lane traffic, blocking all the cars behind.

Everyone honked, deafening my ears. Some whizzed by me
cussing and yelling. The merciless city drivers!
In shock and despair, I sat inside my Mazda giving up the fight.

At A&B Auto Clinic, the doc cleaned her lungs out and said
she was just tired and I should take better care of her.

Next day my Mazda had a heart attack.
The doc insisted it was due to her old age but didn't know
how to cure her. I took her to a specialist in Hollywood.
After a careful examination, the new doc diagnosed that
her gas line was blocked. My Mazda had a by-pass surgery.

The troubles with my Mazda were endless.
One night she conked out on me in the middle of the road again.
This time one wheel came off, nearly killing me.
At last I had to give her up.

As I left her at Honda Yard for a trade, my Mazda shriveled
like an old lady near death. Mazda, everything in this life has
a beginning and end, I consoled. You're not the only one
for this ending. Someday I too may end up in a junkyard
for a trade, hopefully for another life somewhere in the galaxy.

As if Heaven knew the sorrow of our parting, the sky wept
pouring down rain until deep into the night.

At the Mountaintop

At the stroke of the rising sun
the mountain wakes.
My eyes barely open, I breathe
hope.

Such tranquility.

Far away
from the world I chose to live
and struggle in
yet
so near am I
to the memories of that world I cannot
claim as my own.

The sun warm over my head
conquers the mountain in silence
tightly sealed with desert rocks.

Down below, I see
a car passing.
I wonder where it's going . . .

Little flowers whisper good morning
gently mingle with the golden reeds.
Their shadows sway on the rock where
I sit.

At the mountaintop
all worldly concerns seem trivial
yet
I wonder where my life is heading . . .

Consolation

I emptied my brain
laid out
and baked in the Hawaiian sun.

Drenched in sweat
hypnotized by the sound of waves
and the winds
I knew where I stood
for the first time in years.

I threw the sordid words in the ocean
letting them drift away
to be eaten up by fish.

The fattened fish will return
in my dream to build
a seven story paradise where

all my people will have a feast
so unforgettable—
Even the frogs will learn
to laugh at a picnic.

Then I will pass by
the open doors of certain names
with a radiant smile

not cursing
but blessing them all
genuinely like a goddess.

Humiliation

On a beautiful spring afternoon
along the path where the dogwood trees are
lined up, I walk toward the post office.
After the rain, hundreds of buds are
shining in the sun like the faces of
freshly bathed children.

On the pavement I see dead leaves
stepped on numerous times.
I'm reminded of the faces of horror
hunger and anger I saw on television.
Thinking of the war in Iraq
my steps are slow and heavy.

A few feet away in the driveway
a car stops in front of me.
A man, a middle-aged Caucasian
with a face of an angry lion
waves his arm. What does he want?

In a moment, he sticks out his neck
and yells, Go! Go!
No, I'm going this way, I politely answer
and turn into the driveway.
Revving his engine, he shouts
God Bless America!
Not knowing why he's angry at me
I keep on walking.
Again I hear him shout
Smile a little! You, damn foreigner!

Entering the post office
where the American flag is flapping
in the wind, I feel sad and hurt
regretting that I didn't shout back
I am not a foreigner!

My Asian modesty always makes me
look away quietly when I'm confronted
with hostility.

For nearly forty years in America
I've bottled up all the anger from such
humiliations.
My yellow skin and slanted eyes
forever stigmatized
I swallow my pride and turn away
quietly to brood or doodle.
At best I write a few lines of poetry.

Brother

I

Brother
you left your Ma
your children and
your woman
back in Korea.

America is no paradise
you've found out.

You are silent
with no rolling tongue.
You are crippled
with no four-wheeled legs.
And you poison yourself
with regrets.

Cry aloud if you can.
I know you won't.
Instead
you hide and
drown in cigarette smoke.

Sorry
you spilled the ash
by my door yesterday.
Otherwise
I would not have wept
for you.

II

My Brother
slouching your body
lean and weary
you do not jump or sing
as you used to.

I took you out
to my apple tree
last Sunday afternoon.

The sun was high
hidden
behind the cloud screen.

Clinging
to a willowy branch
you chopped and sawed the branches
reaching high to the sky.

Quivering
like a bow against an arrow
you were the leopard
I imagined.

Pour out the stifled breath
of your old memories.
Let it drift away to be the rainfall
in the far away forest.

Mutilated
the apple tree we meant to shape
stood
dumb and crippled.

You said you were sorry
the tree might die.
I said surely
the tree will survive.

America!

('92 L.A. Riots)

America
we have witnessed
your injustice
your indifference
and your violence.

After the King verdict
the torch of rage was lit.
Flames engulfed
the city blocks that we
Korean Americans built
with sweat and blood.

America
you burnt our dreams
to the ground.
Our neighbors became
social bandits
raging
at the crimes you committed.

America
abandoned in the midst
of the inferno
we cried out for your protection.
You never came.

We were left alone
fighting
men and women
young and old
who spilled their anger
in the streets
looting everything
setting fires
shooting—

Even the children joined
rampaging
through the fire storm.

America
desperate to save our lives
our dreams
we picked up sticks and guns
barricading our territory
with carts and automobiles.
We cried for help till dawn

till another sunset.
America
you never came.

All through the night
we heard sirens.
We saw fires erupting
people dying
people gone mad
turning against one another.

Color against color.

America
you left us alone
defenseless
hopeless
betraying our faith in your
democracy.

You taught us violence
against violence.
You betrayed us.
Yet
you ask us to understand
that you never meant to hurt us.

We understand
yes, we do understand now.
Our silence kept us in the corner.
Our lack of smile brought us violence.
Our self-sufficiency created envy and
hatred among our neighbors.

We understand that we are
the scapegoats
in your reckless game.

And now, America
we ask you why—

why you left us alone
with no protection

why you still leave us
with no hope!

Ah, America!
Do you not hear us?
Hear us?

Hear us—!

Some of Us Are Still Wanderers

Some of us
are still wanderers
never finding a home.

Coming from a far country
we are burdened with dreams
shattered
unfulfilled.

Wanting to be home
still
strangely bound
between the parallel
of East and West

many times we sink
to the bottom
and rise
for another beginning
hiding our wounds and anger
from those who accuse us
of our foreignness.

Some of us
drift away from the mainstream
never demanding a connection.

Not knowing
what will become of us
we are driven by fear
for our future
for children.

Our children kill
get killed in the streets
in the ditches
in violence
in despair

while we are running
races in man-made chaos
grasping for our destiny
on borrowed time.

What will become of us?
All of us!

Defenseless
some of us weep in the night
still

wanting
a home.

IV

Passing Love

Epilogue

One day last summer
I woke up with hazy eyes
and saw the sky
gray.

I meant to write poetry.
But no.
For one more doze of magic dream
I buried my head back
in my blue flowered–quilt.

You said
something was wrong
with me.

So, I went
to a homeopathic doctor
for a slice of hope.
She felt my organs in detail
and said my lungs were clogged
my liver weak
my stomach wounded
my kidneys sluggish and
my gall bladder irritated.

In her opinion, I was
defunct.

With an armful of medicines
I walked out of her shack
without telling
that the salty tears of my life
for many years
have made my body deadly.

Next day
when the clock turned
upside down
I sprang up and swung
my limbs to the music
of Janis Joplin.

Melting Camphora 30
at the tip of my tongue
I pressed my lungs
with sentiments like honey.

I drank a glass of Mineral Nectar
soaking
the tissues of my body
to rid the rust and mold.

Wrung
out of my purified blood
surely I thought I could write
poetry then.
But no.
I turned to the mirror and
started to paint my face
instead.

Covered with yellow yolk
running like lava
I lay down on your bed.
By mistake I smiled, wrinkling
my face like a caterpillar skin.

You said
something was terribly wrong
with me.

Peeling off my yellow skin
I walked out of your shelter
without telling

how I'd grown to be sick
living in the shadow
of your majestic pretense
for so many years.

Today
surely I think I can write
poetry.

Spare Me

Your glare
grafting onto my skin
sought the satisfaction
of seeing me beg
for your sympathy.

Mistrust
fattening your curiosity
proved to be
nothing but your
jealousy.

Fear not
for I shall not ask
to share your sourdough.
Such generosity will poison
my sanity in the end.

Spare me
from your twisted mouth
spilling the story
blaming me for your misery
of barrenness.

Spare me
from your glare
your cruelty.

Kindly Speaking

In a perfectly normal manner
I gathered the rainbow of my thoughts.
And in a grand sweeping motion
I laid my laughter
in your gazing curiosity.

I like you, you said.
I see the passion
determination, anger
and frustration underneath
your lovely smile.
Oh, you're capable
of being sweet, submissive
and vulnerable.
I like you, your body, mind
and your Asian sensibility.
I want you—you said.

Curiosity is only a thin skin
of unspoken sin that can be
fermented and disguised
in my smiling silence.

A fool who claims to be a fool
is no fool.
So, don't be fooled by
my silence
my smile
most of all
my Asian sensibility.

Remember

When we first met, remember?
you said what a nice guy you were
what a moral soul you had
unlike Hollywood guys you knew.

When we next met, remember?
you said what a pretty girl I was
what a naive soul I had
unlike Hollywood girls you knew.

I believed you dearly
without knowing the cause or reasons
and we went out for coffee
to be alone, just the two of us.

Then I found out you were not free
with women on a long string
and children calling you Daddy.
I said farewell.

But we met again and again, remember?
feeling happy, feeling sorry—
All along I never thought it was
a game you were used to playing.

You wanted me to stay near you
with a promise that you'd never leave
me alone in the cold winter season.
You loved me then, I thought.

I loved you like a fire and told
you so. It was then your eyes
turned ice cold. You said
you never promised me anything.

The winter is long and lonely.
But never will I call your name, for
I never beg for love.

There's no one in the world
I cannot live without.
When we first met, remember?
I told you so, didn't I?

Love Is

Love is a grave mental disease
said Plato.

Yes, it is.

There is a box in the mental space
for an object to love
one at a time
many at a time.

It grows and grows
like fungus.

Choked up by its own sensation
of madness
it corrodes and dies.

It starts all over again.
From point one.

But why

one never knows what it is
is a disease attained in Mother's womb
to learn

to be alone is impossible for a heart
fed with the blood of life.

Never fulfilled

pumping, always pumping
for more to love
to be loved
all at once, it spreads

indeed
like a disease

within the capacity of mental space
we know nothing about.

Hallucination

I used to hibernate when things went
wrong.
I built thin walls around me
with tears I shed and
fed myself with the air of sighs.

Then things changed.
Through one dark night, I saw
the whole world of my inner self.
My head spinning like spokes
spilled off fragments
of latent memories.

The fire was a stage
with a speck of flame
turning into Disneyland.
The music was an ocean of cries
from the falling dancers.
Off the cliff I fell many a time
into black infinity.

Love, where are you?
I'm with you, taking care of you.
I turned my head quickly
for I saw a lion biting my neck.

Love, where are you?
I'm here, watching you.
I laughed my heart out, for I saw
my love tumbling
over my long black hair.

My face, locked in the mirror
was pale and lifeless.
The tongue was blue
and the neck sharply carved.

Alone
in the dimly lit corridor
of a funeral parlor.
Then

I remembered
things did not change.

Pasted
on a monotonous face of reality
I was the pitiful enemy of my own
world.

Dread

In the heat
I let my mouth spill
the sound of laughter
claiming
the importance
of my presence

violently
wanting to explode

hiding my feelings
my anger and
contempt
toward you who betrayed
me for the security
of your new found pleasure.

Had I known this ending
was to come
I would have prepared
a spare heart
to borrow the time
to heal.

I wanted to murder you
with my sharp tongue
to defy
your superb acting of
such smooth exit.

Instead
I sat on a borrowed bar stool
and laughed haughtily
bleeding
inside my thin skin.

The dusk steals away
my shadow.

I dread
to move
even an inch.

A Masquerade

You called to say goodbye
your angry voice
shooting me down.

I went out
for the Masquerade
in a suicidal mood.

Draped in gray despair
my head bled
bursting
like a bird-pecked pomegranate.

I wore a mask
of the inscrutable.

In the streets of Westwood
night lights blinked.
The eyes of spectators bounced
in fascination.

Halloween.

Clowns hopped around.
Musicians at play strummed
their shoe strings.
Priest and Prostitutes danced
on their toes.
Angels and Devils greeted
with smiles.
KISS, the singing foursome
in painted faces, sauntered
like spiders
into the ice cream parlor.

Clapping.
Laughter.
Enough to bring tears.

A night
to forget fathers and mothers.
A night
to hunt lovers in disguise.
A night
for the old to be children.

Strolling away
from the crowd, I folded
my loneliness in four dollar bills
for a movie, *Days of Heaven*.

In the theater
dark and empty
I peeled off my invisible
mask

a small piece of dream
painted
on my face.

The Footfall

The full moon
glamorized with white
teeth shone
on the pavement.

The dots
zoomed like snowflakes
that winter.

To see you in your lover's arms
is like seeing
a child in his nurse's care.
I'm glad you can now unwind
your lonely breath.
It's a gift.
A memory.

A cat
sitting in the moonlit alley
listened
to my footfall.

Listening to yours
that night I disappeared
into the dark.
If you still remember . . .

How I am tonight
is how you see me.

You will not see
me again.

Passing Love

My head holds a mosaic
filled with intricate thoughts
of many people I've collected
along the paths of my life
over the mountains
across the ocean.

Freely
they come and go
leaving vestiges
scattered like the autumn leaves
in the breeze.

You, my dear one
who happen to be on my palm
this season
can never imagine when
you will be blown away.

Walking along in the dusk
I see marigolds glow; a smile
like yours with the sunray
resting on your face.

How long will it take
till the darkness covers
the flower bed by the road?
How long will the glow
of our love keep on before
storms and fires?

Shall I simply live in an illusion
of moonlight smiles
forgetting the chill in my bones?

A Touch of Love

It wasn't the kind of love I could be proud of
for I could not sing it loudly to you.
Too sick to trust my own existence, I was
touched by your gentle care. Even a whisper
could have melted me down in tears.

The medicines from you were meant to calm my nerves.
Out of gratitude, I sat up for hours into the night
feverishly talking about my stories to you.
As if haunted, it set the fire in me.
It wasn't love, not the kind I could explain.

Bundles of your sympathy packed into my nerves
seeped through the medicines given for my illness.
Soon I was battered by my own misery
instead of getting better as expected.
It wasn't my body that needed to be cured.

It was time for my mind to stand for trials.
For five nights, coughing and spitting out phlegm
I whipped my mind like wintry wind at the hilltop.
Again, I drowned the thoughts of you
in many layered justification.

With no future drawn in my life, I realized
what sculptured me in such nightly torments was
the work of a spirit. Through your smiles
I could clearly see the mistakes and laughed
wildly in my imagination.

Letting You Go

A green face, a green hat
the moon is waning.
The humming of the air purifier is
hypnotic.

The reflection of the light
on the black and white painting is
eclipsed in my eyes.
The plant in the corner is quietly
dying.

Only a dancing elephant
on the antique chest winks at
the spaceship image of his shadow
in the mirror.

No longer in despair
bamboo shoots appear and the plum
flowers come into bloom.
The ghosts are gone and the well is
filled with fresh water
in celebration.

The anticipation of the sunrise
woven into the hours of the night
at last
I've succeeded in letting you go.

V

One Rock, One Pebble, One Moment

A Seagull

Flying
over the middle of the Atlantic Ocean
a seagull finds
an eastward bound ship.

Perched on the deck and fed
by the seamen far from the Orient
the seagull smells the oil
from below.

She flies over and around
the ship as large as a stadium
in a small circle
in a big circle
round and round.

All around the ship, the ocean is
vast and desolate.
In the sky as in a basin
the clouds float around.

In the full moon night
does she miss her family?
When the ship arrives at the shore
will she find her flock?

She flies around the ship
never straying in the Atlantic
fed
by the seamen.

Lost?

In the Sea

The sea at night is an ageless
fathomless sleeping beast
breathing in a steady drone.

Riding on the white foamy waves
the ship, the oil tanker Miriam, glides
with gentle strokes, pumping black fumes
into the sky filled with stars and a silvery moon.

Just a speck on the belly of the sea.

In darkness
I stand on deck, feeling the breeze.
My throat is thick with the poisonous odor of
crude oil from the tank below.
I see nothing but waves
meeting the sky connected in the shadow.

On the face of the sea
a ship of an eighty-five-thousand tons and
a sacrifice of thirty-nine lives on board won't be
enough to prove men are powerful.
Looking into the sea blackened by the depth
of the night, I think of life beyond my own.

Inside the cabin
I cherish small laughter over a glass of wine
rolling in bed after a warm bath.

In this life of the sea, no one is audacious
before God.

Santa Ana Winds

Whistling softly as a flute
Santa Ana winds blew.
At midnight I heard them chatting
with my azalea plants on the balcony.

They flung my door open.
In the sky I saw with awe
seven *Shinsuns* swinging
from south to north
whirling from east to west.
Laughing and singing, they
celebrated their annual outing.
All the while
palm trees sacrificed
their bearings for that
heavenly ritual.

At dawn
devils with scorching breath
perched on the rooftops
in Pacific Palisades. Angry
at Mother Earth, they spilled
their bile, blackening the sky
with charred tongues.

In the morning I heard
the news that many shelters
burnt down, babies were lost
and mothers went mad.

Oh, Santa Ana winds
you let the devils ride with you!

Ojai Retreat

In the night
all is quiet on this mountain side.
Away from the city noises
I'm here to rest and meditate.

In stillness
I hear the raccoon, the visitor
grinding the wood shingles on the roof
rampaging across and back
while I do yoga
to stretch my limbs.

On my desk
the orange-scented flowers keep me
good company.
In a flickering moment of my imagination
I see the ocean through the water
in a blue glass in front of me.

This habit of mine
locking myself up in a room
to converse with God
lays stone steps to my inner journey.

I wonder
where the crescent moon is
hiding behind the heavy drapery
while angels play music
in my ear.

Here in Ojai
I'm to be reached only by God
for all possibilities.

The Scent of an Apple

An apple
red as a red rose

I wash it in the running water
this cold September morning.

Through one bite
my childhood relived

I taste
the sweetness of my youth
the touch of my mother's love

dismissive of
the emptiness
for now.

Pink Clouds

Illuminated by the city lights
in the deep blue ceiling of the night sky
the pink clouds and the full moon played
hide and seek.

My head tilted
I raced the moon and the clouds
quickening my pace on the pavement.

Feeling weightless as if in a space ship
I was an acrobat somersaulting.

      Gathering
      the pink clouds in my hands
      I flipped and skipped
      up and down
      deeper and deeper
      into the sky.

      Playing
      around the moon
      I laughed
      echoing
      like the sound of a gong
      in the heavenly space.

Suddenly
I was blinded by the shadows
of magnolia leaves falling on my face.

Back on the pavement
I quickened my pace.

Entering my room
with an armful of pink clouds
I saw God

the darkness
illuminated.

Huckleberry Picking

With a tin can strung around my neck
I followed
the path in the Northwest woods

picking huckleberries.
Thousands of them
clustered

shining against the blue sky

translucent
they were the red pearls
of the forest.

My wishes and dreams
carefully
picked and packed

I marched down the path
whistling.

Haleakala

Three of us
sailed through the mountain road
to Haleakala crater in Maui.

The sun was setting beyond
the horizon over the hills.
Goats and cows in the countryside
and sugar cane fields all around
we went up and through the winding roads.
With the clouds above
dream houses were scattered miles apart.
The sunset sky was a manifestation
of God's magic.

Veiled with a blanket of clouds
in the Valley Isle
star-like lights twinkled far below.

On top of the mountain
Haleakala at night
the belly of volcanic earth
we embraced the full moon
in one breath.

In ecstasy, we danced with ghosts
hissed like snakes
and gleefully sang like birds
in Paradise.

We were the sole species
in harmony with howling winds
in love with the full moon.

Down in the crater
the miraculous history of the universe
recorded
the darkness and shining light
together held tight.

We knew Pele was pleased.

Night Rain in Maui

The night rain falls
like the falls in Hana
in this Valley Isle
where the sun shines all day.

Bathing
all God's palms
high and low
it washes away the red dust
in the sugar cane fields.

When the night rain swells
enchanted
even the ocean holds its breath
listening to the murmur
of the sky.

In the dark, spirits play
drinking the night rain
splashing ageless laughter
unafraid of demons
pressed under the rocks.

Thoroughly cleansed
everyone and everything
revives
ready for the sunrise.

The Autumn Leaves

Through the long chilly night
I heard the winds bustling
the sky roaring and
the rain knocking on the windows.

The tornado swept through
the Eastern shore.

It was a night for the trees
to endure.

In the morning, I was
awakened by the stroke of the sun
in stillness.
Through the windows, I saw the tree
leaves in such brilliant colors!
Lemon, peach, canary, salmon, crimson
China red, burnt sienna . . . all intermixed
with spotted greens.
Even the sky was limited in my view.

Nature's wonder makes me
contemplate how it all happened
overnight.

Does the endurance bring out
such beauty on trees as it does
to human character?

At the Café, Ace of Cups

(Port Townsend, WA)

After a morning's weeping
the sky has turned calm.

I sit in the Café
Ace of Cups
drinking hot cocoa
listening in tranquility
to the roomful of people.
A home for wanderers
poets, musicians and dreamers.

Fresh cut flowers
on each table.
In the wave of murmurs
smiles float across the room.

On my lap a black kitten sits
content to be friends.

From behind the counter
with homemade pies
Gabriel, the owner, glances over.

Someone's playing piano
my favorite Chopin.

Here at the Café
Ace of Cups by the shore
I forget
yesterday's pain
tomorrow's concern.

Now I know why one goes
mad in the city
freezing in loneliness
closing the doors to all
even to oneself.

One Rock, One Pebble, One Moment

Picking up the pebbles
on the beach
I met a man with a dog.

What you got there?
He smiled and asked.

Pebbles, I said.

What you got there?
I asked, looking at
a rock in his hand
large as a seagull.

A rock, he said.

What for?
I questioned.

For my garden.
He chuckled.

One at a time?

He nodded.

One rock
One pebble
One moment

of happiness
is
one step toward
Heaven.

VI

Falling In Love

With You Away

How glad I am you've come back.
Alone I cried like a haunted soul
in an empty tomb.

With you away, the world closed
on me silently, and I heard the air
whispering to the wall.

The telephone sat mutely in the corner.
Aimlessly, I walked in my shadow
of desolation, neglecting everything.

I'm sorry you've found your fish dead
the plants wilted, and the needle of
your record player stuck on the track

cut deep in its own circle.
All along, my eyes sat in a well
famished by the absence of you.

One Spring Day

The golden sun, the blue soul
over the eternal wave, unseen
it is the sign of birth
Pisces, this spring day.

Morning
visit to Bon and Strom:
       A forest of carnival garments
       the mounds of trick sales
       the drawn wax museum of Simplicity.

       A freckled lady raved about the wonder
       of Eternal 27
       calling her crinkled skin a miracle.

       I stuffed my shrunk stomach
       with a bell taco, then sailed through
       a labyrinth of frantic red and green
       traffic eyes.

       At school, a teacher slipped words
       through his sun-burnt lips, blaming
       the season of spring.

Afternoon
shopping at the U District:
       Books on showcases
       a glass jar with a tight-lipped Italian mouth
       a poster of trees with an illusion of life
       a worn-out wall calendar at half price and
       a map of the world to measure how small
       one could be.

Evening
sun down under a magnolia tree:
        A frozen smile blossoms followed by
        a feast of eight ordinary vegetables
        on a painted table.
        The cut strawberries turned bloody
        in the refrigerator.

        The weary husband self-diagnosed his fate
        "despondent," eating the half-torn
        prestige as a professor.
        Humped over, he sat on a couch
        grumbling, "Only two percent raise—"

The moon, the white soul
over the infinite void
it is an exchange of smiles
life, this spring night.

The Fog Horn

(Port Townsend, WA)

The night deepened
veiling the slumbering earth.
A fog horn wailed
far from the island.

He and I
the strangers who met
only yesterday
by the eyes
liking the sunshine
on the grass . . .
We were walking
into the forest.

    Trees, oh trees
    ever so green evergreen
    trees, I whispered.
    Your heads plunged
    deeply
    into the sky far above
    you embrace my heart
    as no man.

Out in the clearing,
we swam through the fog
blooming
white.

We stood, listening.
The fog horn wailed.

Faintly in the distance
we heard crickets chirping
dogs barking and the ocean
waves slapping the shore
through the seaweed breeze.

In stillness
we were twins in the womb
of Mother Earth.

My hair curled up wet
seasoned with the salty breeze.
His hands slowly drew
my face to his, brushing my hair
with his gentle breath.

On the dark sand
we left our footprints.
Our time together already
washed away

strangers we were
unseen
like the fog
one summer night.

       I hear the thrashing sound
       of his footsteps
       fading
       into the breath of my memory.
       I hear
       the fog horn echoing
       in my ears.
       And I remember

the trees
ever green
everlasting . . .

In the Shadow

Your eyes
shadowed by the weight
of an impossible love, you dream
to wander like the autumn breeze.

The picture of your man
lonely as a mountain goat
smiles in your direction.

In the memory of meeting him
in the snowy mountain ridge
five miles away from his homestead

you see him in the shadow of your eyes
dancing in slow motion
to the tune of blues.

You wait
for the affirmation of your fate
next summer.

Allow Me

If I must worry about how
I will live in my old age
without wealth
I would be without health now
and how can I live to be
old?

If I must worry about how
I will live in my old age
without love
I would be without dreams now
and how can I go on living
another day?

Allow me to sit in the sun
and listen to the sky.
I will love you gently.

Allow me to stay in my room
and weave my rainbows.
I will love you truly.

Like a colt in the meadow
with no boundary
allow me

to wander around

till I hear the autumn
stealthily
strolling by my door.

I will be waiting
to be with you
then.

Autumn by Lake Superior

In the lake
the reflection of sunset
tirelessly dances in the waves.

The wind blows with a gentle whistle.
The autumn leaves fall
like flying birds
or Chinese acrobats in slow motion.
Some land on the grass, making
the patches of a quilt in yellow, orange
and red.

A few prefer floating on the water.
In the shimmering waves
they surrender
to the moments of pleasure in peace.

In this cottage by Lake Superior
I count no days to come
no days gone by.

I am simply here now
content
with the man who loves me
as if I were a newborn.

Falling in Love

Like a leafless tree
in an empty courtyard

without you
I was

seized by lonely cries
of the wind.

To find a direction
for such vacant feelings
I went out to the street

and wandered.

In an embrace
of an old friend
I spilled laughter
like broken beads falling
on a tin pan.

Alone
in the night, I fell
deeply into nostalgia
of autumn
by the lake.

Love is not, I know
a sentimental journey
but the heart's choice
for a life in togetherness.

I will no longer be
a thorn bird.

A Private Moment

The hum of the refrigerator
the bellowing sound of the heater
and the whisper of the fountain

all blended with the sound of
my love's snoring which he calls
the sign of his clear conscience

make my private moment
of the night
precious.

Being in Love

Awakened from a dream, I curl up
and turn. The roses on the dresser
smile and your words bloom.
The red roses for Valentine's Day.

Like in a film
thoughts of you unfold
moment by moment.

I vaguely hear
the sound of your spoon scooping cereal
the water stream in the shower
the buzzing noise of your electric razor
like a singing of a cicada.

Your footsteps in and out of the bedroom.
Your lips touching my cheek lightly.
And the sound of the door shutting.

In your light
I fall asleep again under the warm quilt
happily like a child.

Upon waking
on the kitchen counter I find a half
grapefruit carefully cut and sectioned.
Such a loving touch is a milestone
for my newly found happiness.

VII

As My Life Is A Dream

Reflections in the Window

After midnight
my typewriter records the sound
of the ocean
beyond the shoulder of bougainvillea.

I see my limbs tangled
in the reflection on the window pane.
For future reference
I keep on drawing them until my eyes
and hands become tangled
in the reflection of the space
to see through what seems to be
impossible to see.

Perhaps
my eyes are keener than my ears
my hand sharper than my tongue.
In that case I'd say
draw on the paradise
instead of telling the stories of hell.

But no. I'm waiting
still waiting for the gush of words
to flow, to glide
like smoke from the chimney
like the tropical shower.

Sea grapes, fan trees and coconut groves
tell me what the sea breeze murmurs
tickling you.

Be kind to me.
I have no friends to sing with
for I have to be all things to myself.

Emptiness

There is no place to hide
no one to turn to.

Drowning in the river
of despair

you forget the smell of roses
from one moment past.

You are not alone.

Amongst the crowd
milling around
like cattle in the thunder storm

buzzing about in the crater of
chaos
you are not alone.

In the space
your body occupies
on this earth
you feel the hollowness
inside you
circling in echo.

So you vomit
the soundless cry
the shapeless despair
curling like a dying grapevine
dissolved
till you hit the bottom
of a fathomless pit.

In nothingness
you no longer grope
for life.

In that moment
of emptiness

the grace of God reaches
your heart

opening
the road to eternal bliss
of another illusion

for another life.

You embrace the emptiness
within you
entering the world of love
amongst the crowd.

Only then
your future is led on.

Searching

I chuckle at myself
my fluid emotion
my babbling words
my itchy body
like waves
big
and small

always restless.

I try hard to reach out
way out there
somewhere
and in
all the way
into my soul.

In one moment
tears flood my heart.
In another
a roaring laughter escapes.

Lost
in my own cleverness

forever speculating about today
and tomorrow
I talk much, think much, dream much
till
I collapse
exhausted
folding my weary body
into one knot.

Oh dear God
when can I ever cease this prayer?

The Final Contemplation

The time has come to sit down and contemplate.
Let the marchers go into the street and beat their drums
and scream to the top of the hills.
The villagers will gather around the courtyard to watch
the hanging man dance to the tune of the rap song
before the dawn.

When the rain falls, the mountain spirits will descend
to take the dead to the gate of the Immortal Zone.
The mourners left behind will stay flat to the ground
unable to pick up their broken hearts.

That will pass in a flickering moment
like the sound of laughter hanging in the air.
Memories will fade like an age-old family photo.
In the end, all living and dead will meet in the Milky Way
for the final contemplation.

In A Cycle

I collect memories of many faces
especially those
dead.

Creating a life of its own
each dwells in a block of
cells.

Death, after all, is
living memories
in the space

of our thoughts
kept
in the universe where nothing
disappears
but
everything is reflected
in ways
unknown to us.

Life and death are together
in a cycle
as light and darkness.

Yet
when our loved ones die
we fear for our own
separation.

Living in Dreams

In Lake Gibbs, Washington
I met some people who lived
out in the woods.

Building a boat in the forest
they lived in dreams.
Some day we wanna sail way
around the world
said a man, brightly smiling.
In his eyes, blue as the ocean
I saw the sails flapping.
The children looked up at him
with angelic smiles.
In their eyes, blue as the sky
I saw the mirror to a magician's door.

In Hollywood, California
I knew some people who lived
on the city boulevard.

Slaving themselves to their careers
they too lived in dreams.
Some day we wanna buy a big house
and a fancy Cadillac
said a man proudly grinning.
He was a janitor, his wife a nurse.
The children watched the house
killing time with toys and guns.
In their eyes, cold as the snow
I saw deer at the hunter's ritual.

Whichever way I dream, I know
one thing for sure
to keep my heart centered in God.

The Mirror

The mirror of my soul
never breaks

knowing
the simple wisdom

that life goes on

with
or
without

my reflection.

Summoned

We are the saints
fallible
with no halos

summoned
to give others what we have
and have not received
completely.

Glamour of nihilism and
violence
celebrated by our children
as new age aesthetics
is killing us all.

Forgetting
we live by grace
not by our aspirations and
desires
to perfect our lives
we are lost
in the wilderness of
human madness.

Summoned
for a new life
let us embrace our
saintliness
however fallible
it may be.

In Pure Joy

Inactive
one can die
with no harm done.

Active
one can march
to death
not knowingly.

If I have a sweet cup
of magic
now
I'll make all the sick
laugh

and
laugh
in pure joy.

On the Freeway

Alongside the freeway
a poppy field is seen
in a short stretch.

In the brilliant May sun
the color of the bright red
almost translucent
darts into my eyes
warming my heart
with nostalgia.

I find my mother's garden
hidden inside my memory lane
for the first time
since her death
twenty years ago.

How time has fled
in the freeway of my destiny
along with the fragments of

memories
conveniently filed away
for daily survival.

As My Life is a Dream

I painted a phoenix in bright colors
cut it in nine pieces and cooked it
in a pot at the mountaintop.
I stirred it as if cranking reels of
a movie. Unraveled were a series
of faces in mosaic.

Kurosawa appeared. He asked me
what my story was about.
Tongue-tied, I could not answer.
He handed me a token with a silvery
eagle engraved, ready to fly.

How real I thought everything was
in my dream!

In my waking hour, I see
the remnant of the war between
my head and heart.

Now in cease-fire, my chest is filled
with the fresh breeze of serenity.
I begin to breathe gently as my story
is unraveled like in a movie.

No longer haunted, my love of God soars
as I see my guardian angel smile
in the clear blue sky, transforming to
one gigantic phoenix.

My wandering in the wilderness of
the mind has taught me a little wisdom.
I believe my dreams are real
as my life is a dream.

Returning

Thoughts are nurtured
by the touch of my soul.

Born out of thoughts
words are made to be beads.

I string them to capture
the memories of time
spent in this life

returning

somewhere in the universe
to be imprinted in the void

like stars.

A New Life

The root of my ego was spread too thin
    easily shaken and damaged
        with branches drooped over the rocky ground.

Too heavy to hold, my back was bent.
    I was doomed to cut down the old and dead
        branches, which blinded my view all around.

My faint prayers are to be answered now
    and the new sprouts will spring from within
        my self, strongly rooted in my center.

About the Author

Born and raised in South Korea, Chungmi Kim came to America with a B.A. in English from Ewha University in Seoul. She earned an M.A. in Theater Arts from U.C.L.A. and has participated in the Warner Bros Minority Writers Program for Television, WGA Open Door Writing Program, the Mark Taper Forum's Mentor Playwrights Program and USC Professional Writing Program.

Chungmi—Selected Poems was her first book. Her Poetry has appeared in numerous anthologies, magazines, journals, on a spoken word CD, and in Los Angeles buses as part of the Poetry Society of America's *Poetry In Motion LA '98-'99 Project*.

Awards she has received include the first place Open Door Writing Award for her screenplay, *The Dandelion*, from the Writers Guild Foundation, West and Grand Prize for her play, *The Comfort Women*, at the 1995 USC One-Act Play Festival. In 1999, her full-length play, *Hanako*, had a world premiere at East West Players in Los Angeles. For television, her credits include writing and producing *The Koreans In L.A.* and *Poets In Profile* for KCET-TV. As Co-Producer of *Korea: The New Power in the Pacific*, a one-hour documentary for KCBS-TV, she received an Emmy nomination.

She currently resides in Falls Church, Virginia.